KU-167-720

This book belongs to:

_____

A catalogue record for this book is available from the British Library

Published by Ladybird Books Ltd
A Penguin Company
Penguin Books Ltd, 80 Strand, London WC2R 0RL, UK
Penguin Books Australia Ltd, Camberwell, Victoria, Australia
Penguin Group (NZ) Ltd, 67 Apollo Drive, Rosedale, North Shore 0632, New Zealand

2 4 6 8 10 9 7 5 3
© LADYBIRD BOOKS LTD MCMXCVIII. This edition MMVI

ISBN-13: 978-1-84422-931-4

Printed in China

Thumbelina

illustrated by Jane Kochnewitz

Once upon a time, there was a woman who had no children. What the woman really wanted was a little girl.

One day, an old woman came to see her.

"Plant this seed," said the old woman. "Soon you will have a little girl."

So the woman planted the seed, and very soon, there was a flower. When the flower opened, out came a little girl. The woman took the little girl into her home.

"You are as little as my thumb," said the woman. "So I shall call you Thumbelina."

The woman looked after Thumbelina, and Thumbelina was happy.

One day, a toad saw
Thumbelina playing.

"What a pretty little girl!"
said the toad. "I shall take
her home with me. She will
marry my son."

So the toad hopped up to
Thumbelina and took her
away to the pond. She left
Thumbelina on a lily leaf
and went to look for her son.

But Thumbelina wasn't very happy. She didn't want to marry a toad. She wanted to be back home with her mother.

Just then, a butterfly flew by.

"Please help me," said Thumbelina. "The toad wants me to marry her son, but I don't want to. I want to go home."

19

The butterfly flew down to
the lily leaf. Thumbelina
jumped onto the butterfly's
back, and they flew to
a wood.

Thumbelina was very happy in the wood. She stayed there all summer. But when winter came, all the butterflies flew away. Thumbelina was all alone.

A mouse came by.

"Please help me," said Thumbelina. "I'm cold and I don't have a home."

The mouse said, "Come and live with me."

The winter was very long and very cold.

"Soon there will be no more food for you," said the mouse. "The old mole has food. He is coming to see us today. Why don't you marry him?"

But Thumbelina wasn't very happy. She didn't want to marry the old mole and she didn't want to live down in a dark tunnel.

When the mole came
he said, "Come and see
my little home in the tunnel.
You will be happy there."

So Thumbelina went to see
the old mole's home.

31

In the mole's tunnel,
Thumbelina saw a swallow
who was hurt.

"All of my friends flew away
when winter came," said the
swallow. "I'm all alone."

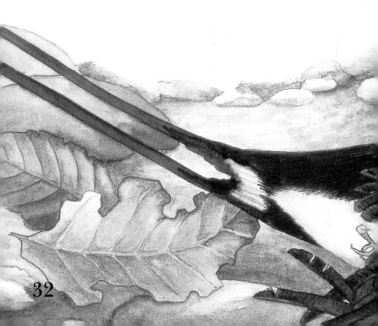

Thumbelina looked after the swallow all winter. When summer came, the swallow was better and he flew away to be with his friends.

Once more Thumbelina was left alone.

"Soon it will be winter again. I will have to marry the old mole and live down in his dark tunnel."

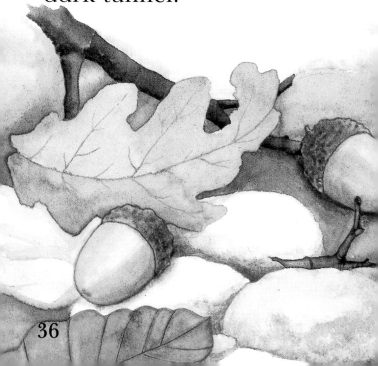

Just then, Thumbelina's swallow flew down to her.

"Come with me," he said. "I will take you to the land of summer."

So Thumbelina jumped onto the swallow's back, and they flew away.

The land of summer was full of flowers. In each of the flowers lived a little boy or girl, just like Thumbelina.

"Come and live with us," they said.

They took Thumbelina to see
their prince.

The Prince said, "Will you
marry me, Thumbelina?"

And Thumbelina said, "Yes."

So Thumbelina and the
Prince lived happily
ever after.

Read It Yourself is a series of graded readers designed to give young children a confident and successful start to reading.

Level 3 is suitable for children who are developing reading confidence and stamina, and who are ready to progress to longer stories with a wider vocabulary. The stories are told simply and with a richness of language.

About this book

At this stage of reading development, it's rewarding to ask children how they prefer to approach each new story. Some children like to look first at the pictures and discuss them with an adult. Some children prefer the adult to read the story to them before they attempt it for themselves. Many children at this stage will be eager to read the story aloud to an adult at once, and to discuss it afterwards. Unknown words can be worked out by looking at the beginning letter (*what sound does this letter make?*) and the sounds the child recognises within the word. The child can then decide which word would make sense.

Developing readers need lots of praise and encouragement.